Lee Gold's sense of adventure has led her to the Cordon Bleu cooking school in London, the restaurants of Paris, the markets of Hong Kong and ten years in New York where she ran her own cookery school and catering service. She was also an integral part of the world-famous Macy's culinary team. Lee has blended these international experiences with her own health-oriented approach to today's cooking.

She lives in Sydney with her husband and two sons.

Also by Lee Gold

*Food in a Flash*
*Jewish Cooking*
*Fat Fighting Foods*
*Hormone Health*
*High Speed Low Fat*
*Anti-ageing—the Secrets*

# 7 Day
# Health
# and Vitality
# Plan

**Including 50 body-cleansing recipes**

# Lee Gold

PAN BOOKS

The information in this book is intended to be a general
nutritional guide for people seeking to improve their health.
Anyone suffering from a physical disorder should only follow
the advice in this book under their doctor's supervision.

First published 2001 by Pan Macmillan Australia Pty Limited

This edition published 2002 by Pan Books
an imprint of Pan Macmillan Ltd
Pan Macmillan, 20 New Wharf Road, London N1 9RR
Basingstoke and Oxford
Associated companies throughout the world
www.panmacmillan.com

ISBN 0 330 42036 4

Copyright © Pan Macmillan Australia Pty Limited 2001

1 3 5 7 9 8 6 4 2

A CIP catalogue record for this book is available from
the British Library

Printed and bound in Great Britain by
Mackays of Chatham plc, Chatham, Kent

# Contents

# Introduction

It is vitally important to make time for your health and for yourself. The best form of life insurance you can have is to take responsibility for your health. Most of us know what aspects of our health and lifestyle we need to change, but think that it is too hard to do what is required. However, it is not as hard as we often think. By making quite small changes to our lives we can dramatically improve them and our personal health.

The hardest part of making lifestyle changes is getting motivated. But it is always easier to maintain motivation when the task is achievable. Because the 7 day health and vitality plan is just that—one week—anyone should be able to stick to it. It is also full of motivational ideas and delicious recipes that will help you stick to the plan.

The 7 day health and vitality plan improves your health by cleansing, nourishing and resting the body. It is a safe and effective plan that kick-starts your body's own healing mechanisms and will help bring your body back to the peak of health within a relatively short period of time.

The rewards are fairly immediate—it's amazing how quickly our bodies can repair themselves once we give them a chance—and include benefits such as:

- glowing skin
- weight loss
- good body tone
- higher energy levels
- being less susceptible to stress
- loss of cellulite
- a feeling of relaxation and calmness

The 7 day health and vitality plan lasts for just a week but the benefits to your health continue for a lot longer. It is not expensive or difficult to do. Unlike diets, where you are starving your body, on the 7 day health and vitality plan you will be fuelling your body, following delicious recipes that are designed to cleanse you from within. It also helps you learn how to care for your body in other ways and to look after your emotional needs.

Think of the 7 day health and vitality plan as a 'spring-cleaning' of the body; a chance to rid it of the build up of excess waste and toxins accumulated over the years. It will help protect your body from disease, restore and enhance vitality, allow you to look your best and ensure your ability to maintain optimum health.

If you want to take control of your health, have more energy and feel younger, then you are ready for the 7 day health and vitality plan. Let's begin!

# 1

# All about
# health
# and
# vitality

# Why do we lose our health and vitality?

In the modern world our lifestyles are slowly clogging up and 'poisoning' our bodies. We pollute our air. We don't drink enough water. We eat the wrong kinds of food. We don't get enough sleep or exercise. We smoke, drink too much alcohol and consume too much caffeine. All of these factors slowly add up and start to have an effect on our bodies—although the human body is very adaptable, eventually it will become overloaded.

Your body is a highly sophisticated structure that is designed to maintain an internal balance. It uses foods and fluids for nourishment, repair and maintenance. Your organs and internal systems then process these, and your body keeps what it needs, eliminating the waste and by-products.

Elimination of waste is a natural process that is constantly occurring. However, when the natural balance is upset, things can start to go wrong. This is when your body needs some extra help from you. You don't need to see a doctor to know when your health is not at its best, because your body will tell you. You can take stock of your wellbeing every day by simply taking a look in the mirror.

If you suffer from any of the following symptoms your body is crying out for help:

- indigestion
- irritable bowel syndrome
- headaches
- tiredness
- sugar cravings
- allergies
- bad breath
- irritability
- sleep problems
- poor skin condition

# How does the 7 day health and vitality plan work?

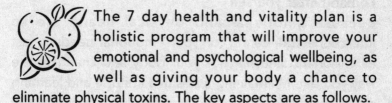 The 7 day health and vitality plan is a holistic program that will improve your emotional and psychological wellbeing, as well as giving your body a chance to eliminate physical toxins. The key aspects are as follows.

## Changing the way you eat

This does not mean going hungry! By fuelling your body with pure, natural and nourishing foods that are easy to digest, you are giving it a chance to cleanse itself from within. There is no limit to the amount of food you can eat; you just focus on helpful foods rather than harmful ones.

## Exercising

Exercise is one of the fastest ways to improve your health, gain more energy and feel better about yourself. It also helps you lose weight and tone your body, as well as speeding up your metabolism. You do not have to become a gym junkie or get up at the crack of dawn every day to enjoy the benefits of exercise—30 minutes a day is all you need.

## Caring for your body

This includes massage, exfoliation, dry-skin brushing and water therapy. Caring for your body helps to speed up your metabolism, gives you more energy, and makes you look and feel great.

## Looking after yourself

Because emotional and physical health are so interconnected, caring for your emotional needs is just as important as caring for your body and changing the way you eat. Maintaining a positive attitude and learning stress management and relaxation techniques are the key to emotional health.

With the 7 day health and vitality plan you are not trying to change a lifetime's habits overnight; you are merely taking a week out to give your body a chance to rest and recover. However, you can use it to start implementing some long-term changes. You can utilise the 7 day health and vitality plan as a guideline for good health, incorporating its principles into your daily life. You can also use the plan as a pick-me-up or whenever you feel that your state of health needs an extra boost.

However you decide to use it, the 7 day health and vitality plan will give your body the help it needs to cleanse itself and bring you to optimum health. The results of the plan far outweigh the effort you will put into it, and you will be amazed at the difference just one week can make.

# 2

# Changing
## the way
## you eat

# Why is it so hard to change eating habits?

 Why do so many diets fail? Why do people keep on eating foods they know are harmful to their bodies? And why do people still feel hungry when they have already eaten more than enough?

The simple answer is because people eat for a lot of reasons other than satisfying hunger and getting nutrition. We all do this at some point or another, especially in times of stress, when our bodies really need healthy foods.

The first step to changing your eating habits is to look at the real reasons why you are eating. Do any of the following reasons sound familiar to you?

**Nurturing and self-reward**
Nurturing is something that is tied into our basic survival instincts—a mother's instinct to feed her children is incredibly powerful—and so from an early age most people associate food with love. When we grow up this often becomes self-nurturing—we feed ourselves when we crave this type of unconditional mother's love. This is why we often use food as a personal reward to help motivate ourselves, for example, when we are trying to meet a deadline at work or studying for an exam. Most food is cheap (especially junk food) and accessible to

everyone, and it is an immediate reward that feels good.

## To fill emotional hunger
We often use food as a substitute for love, friends or success. Emotional hunger can easily be confused with physical hunger when we feel unloved, unwanted or unrecognised.

## Social and cultural reasons
Coffee, alcohol and food are all a part of our culture. We go out to dinner, to the pub or to have coffee so that we can catch up with family and friends. Eating and drinking bring groups of people together.

## Habits and addictions
Alcohol and caffeine are both highly addictive, and we often consume tea, coffee, chocolate and alcohol because our bodies are craving these substances. Many people who are addicted to caffeine suffer headaches if they miss their caffeine fix.

# How do you change eating habits?

 Once we understand why we eat we can start making changes to our lifestyles and improvements to our emotional health that will result in long-term changes to our physical health. Here are some ideas.

## Substitute tastes and textures

If you are not yet ready to deal with the emotional issues behind your eating, you can change your eating habits by replacing body-clogging foods with body-cleansing substitutes. This way you will not go hungry, and by filling your body with good foods your physical sensation of fullness will help to counteract your emotional hunger. There is a list of these on page 23.

## Nurturing and self-reward

The best way to tackle this type of eating is to substitute something else for food. Save up the money you would normally spend on junk food and instead buy yourself a book, a CD, a piece of clothing, makeup or some beautiful body treatments. The idea is still to indulge and reward yourself, but to do it with something other than food.

## Emotional hunger

If you are eating to satisfy emotional hunger, you need to start addressing the emotional issues behind your eating before you can change your eating habits. Talk to your GP or find a good counsellor who can help you deal with these issues. There are also plenty of great self-help books on the market that can assist you. When you are ready, start to talk to those you love about your issues.

## Social and cultural reasons

You can still use food as a tool to catch up with family and friends while you are on the 7 day health and vitality plan. There are many healthy menu options available at restaurants. Try suggesting new places to catch up where there is a large selection of foods (Asian restaurants are a great example) and you can have your fill of healthy ones. Explain to friends who don't support your new choice in eating why you are changing your habits and, if necessary, avoid eating with those who try to pressure you into unhealthy food choices. If you are cooking for the family, try some new, healthier recipes that everyone can enjoy.

## Habits and addictions

These are hard to change but it can be done. You can either go cold turkey (it helps if you do it with a friend or your partner) or slowly reduce your levels of caffeine and/or alcohol, replacing them with substitutes as you go. For caffeine addicts, there are wonderful brands of tea that taste just like normal caffeinated tea but have less than three per cent caffeine. Ask for them at your local health-food shop. There are also some delicious decaffeinated coffees around and most cafes now serve these. Alcohol addiction will probably need some professional help but if you are just a social consumer, avoiding pubs and trying some non-alcoholic cocktails and mixes will help.

# Why should you change the way you eat?

You need to change the way you eat to help your body cleanse itself. Changing your eating habits is the fastest and easiest way to good health and long life. Food is a natural and very powerful medicine; it has the power both to prevent disease and to heal our bodies. Once you start to think of food as a type of medicine you will realise just how important it is to fill your body with good food.

Healthy eating is the core of the 7 day health and vitality plan. It will flush the toxins out of your body and leave you feeling revitalised and squeaky-clean. You will not feel hungry when you are eating healthy foods.

The basic idea of healthy eating is to eat foods that are as unrefined and unprocessed as possible. These types of foods are easy to digest, they give you energy and help the process of internal body cleansing.

While you are on the 7 day health and vitality plan you need to:

1. Avoid or eat less of the 'body-clogging' foods – those that are hard to digest or are overprocessed.
2. Eat more of the 'body-cleansing foods' – those that are easy to digest and good for you.
3. Take natural supplements that will help your body cleanse itself.
4. Increase water consumption.

# What should you eat?

**'Body-clogging' foods**

While you are cleansing your body certain foods will need to be avoided. These will slow down your digestion and place an extra workload on your organs of elimination, thereby hindering your body-cleansing process.

- RED MEAT
  Meat takes a long time for the body to digest, placing a huge workload on the digestive system. Non-organic meat may also contain traces of hormones.

- ALCOHOL AND CAFFEINE
  These substances are products that the body cannot absorb. The liver has to break them down and they add to the levels of waste in the body. Alcohol and caffeine also dehydrate the body.

- DAIRY PRODUCTS
  These are usually high in fat. Also, lactose (milk sugar) can be difficult to digest. However, acidophilus yoghurt can be consumed while on the 7 day health and vitality plan as it is easy to digest and is full of 'good' bacteria that help cleanse your insides and eliminate the 'bad' bacteria that live in your gut.

- GLUTEN-CONTAINING GRAINS
  These include wheat, rye, barley and oats. Gluten (found in flour made from these grains) can be difficult to digest.

- SUGAR, SUCROSE AND GLUCOSE
  These are basically empty kilojoules, with little or no nutritional value. They also will make your blood sugar levels rise and fall very quickly. Chocolate contains caffeine, dairy products and refined sugars, so it is way up there on the 'no' list.
- PRE-PACKAGED, FAST AND/OR HEAVILY PROCESSED FOODS
  Most of the goodness has been removed from these foods, and they are usually laden with fat, sugar and salt.
- CONDIMENTS SUCH AS SALT, TOMATO SAUCE, MAYONNAISE AND CHUTNEY
  Condiments often contain a lot of salt. High blood pressure, potassium deficiency and water retention are all side effects of too much salt. There is enough salt in the foods we eat without adding it as a condiment.

Rather than having big meals, it is better to eat smaller portions more frequently, as this speeds up your metabolism and you are less likely to feel hungry.

### 'Body-cleansing' foods

The following foods are all excellent sources of nutrition and are easy to digest. They will fuel your body to its maximum vitality and health. Eat plenty of these foods every day and try to have as wide a variety of them as possible. See the back of this book for some delicious recipes using 'body-cleansing' foods.

- VEGETABLES

These are high in nutrients and fibre, contain very little waste and very few kilojoules. Vegetables are best eaten raw, as raw foods contain a higher percentage of dietary fibre and clean the gut more efficiently. If you want to eat your vegetables cooked, steam or microwave, rather than boil them. When you boil your vegetables you loose most of the goodness, as it ends up in the cooking water.

Another excellent way of cooking vegetables is to bake them in the oven with their skins on. Most of the goodness in vegetables is found in or near the skin, so try to eat them with their skin.

The vegetables that are especially good for you are the antioxidant-rich ones, such as carrots, sweet potatoes, beetroot and leafy greens. Antioxidants defend the body against free radical damage, and can prevent cancer, degenerative diseases and ageing. You need a variety of antioxidants in order for them to do their job properly, and this is why it is important to eat a variety of fruit and vegetables. The 7 day health and vitality plan is a great time to try some new vegetables that you have never eaten before.

- FRUIT

Fruit, like vegetables, is high in fibre, nutrients, and essential vitamins and minerals. Fruit also has a high water content and is an excellent source of natural sugar. When you are craving something sweet, fruit is a wonderful substitute for refined sugar products.

Dried fruit makes the ideal snack, as it is totally portable and high in energy.

- FISH

  Fish is an excellent food that is easy to digest. While all varieties of fish contain essential proteins, oily fish (such as salmon, tuna, trout and sardines) also contains essential fatty acids. Fresh fish is the best and has the most nutrients, however, frozen and canned fish are still okay. If you are buying canned fish, get it in oil, rather than brine, which has a high salt content.

- PULSES AND LEGUMES

  These are high in nutrients and vitamins. Freshly sprouted seeds are easiest to digest. Sprouts and seeds are full of flavour, and are a great way to add extra variety and nutrients to your diet. Try chickpeas, pumpkin seeds (great as a snack), alfalfa and lentils.

- RICE

  Rice helps to clean out your gut as it travels through your body because it is very absorbent. It is also very easy to digest and very filling. Try to eat a variety of rice, such as arborio (great for risotto), wild rice, basmati and brown rice. Brown rice is the best rice for you because it is less refined than white rice. This means it has more fibre and it contains more nutrients than the highly refined varieties. It is also the most absorbent.

- HERBS AND SPICES

  These are primarily used to add flavour to foods but they often have medicinal properties as well. Garlic and ginger are especially good for you and will add a lot of flavour, as will chilli, rosemary, pepper, parsley and coriander. Experiment with some herbs and spices that you may not have tried before.

- CHEESE, MILK AND YOGHURT
  Just because you have to avoid most dairy foods doesn't mean that you can't enjoy cheese, milk and yoghurt. Acidophilus yoghurt is full of 'good' bacteria and it helps you cleanse your gut of 'bad bacteria'. There are some wonderful 'non-dairy' products available today that are easier to digest than those made from cow's milk. Some of the foods made from sheep and goat's milk actually stimulate digestion. Try drinking sheep's milk, goat's milk, soy milk or rice milk. There are also some delicious cheeses and yoghurts that are made with sheep and goat's milk.

- OTHER FOODS (NUTS, OILS, SEEDS, OLIVES, MUSTARD, SEAWEED, TAHINI, TOFU)
  These all add flavour and variety to your diet. Nuts are high in kilojoules but are an excellent source of essential fatty acids. They are also very high in nutrients and make an excellent snack food, especially when combined with dried fruit. Nuts should be eaten raw and unsalted. Olive and seed oils are very good for you.

- FOODS TO EAT IN MODERATION
  Chicken and eggs should be eaten in moderation because they are harder to digest and are higher in fats and cholesterol than the body-cleansing foods. However, as they contain many essential nutrients

they are okay in small doses. Try to eat only free-range chicken and eggs as they are less likely to contain traces of hormones. Try not to eat more than two eggs a week.

## Natural supplements

These supplements will enhance the effect of the 7 day health and vitality plan. They are not an essential part of the program, and do not have to be taken every day, but you will find they do speed up and enhance the process of body cleansing.

- LIVER TONICS

  Hot lemon water is excellent for your liver. A squeeze of fresh lemon juice in a cup of hot water is a great way to start your day. Apart from hot lemon water, other liver tonics include fresh garlic cloves, black grapes, fennel or dandelion tea, and fresh carrot and beetroot juice.

- KIDNEY TONICS

  These include honey in hot water, fresh melon and fresh cranberries or cranberry juice.

- KELP SUPPLEMENTS

  Kelp contains iodine, which keeps the metabolic rate steady. This is especially important when we change our eating habits, and so taking kelp will prevent your metabolism dropping while you are on the plan.

## The importance of water consumption

Water consumption is crucial to the 7 day health and vitality plan. Our bodies consist of 80 per cent water and we need to maintain those water levels. If your body is not getting enough water it will attempt to take fluids from your bowel. This dries out your faeces, making it slower and harder for them to move out of the body. When intestinal waste takes a long time to move through the bowel, toxins are reabsorbed back into the bloodstream through the intestinal wall. Side effects include constipation and hemorrhoids.

In order to maintain the correct water levels you need to drink two litres of water a day. This is about eight glasses. An easy way of ensuring that you drink this amount is to buy a two-litre jug and fill it up first thing every morning. Leave it in a prominent place so that every time you see it you are reminded to have another drink. Continue to drink from this jug until it is all gone, making sure that you finish it before going to bed every night.

Try to use bottled or filtered water where possible, but tap water is fine if you can't get these. If you crave soft drinks, drink sparkling mineral water. Try hot water or herbal teas instead of tea or coffee. And if you are looking for an extra tang, squeeze some fresh lemon or lime juice into your glass of water. Before you know it, drinking water will become a pleasant habit and you will not be missing soft drinks, or tea or coffee.

## Body-cleansing substitutes

As discussed earlier, it is often very hard to change eating habits, especially if they are tied into emotional factors. One of the simplest ways to get on to the right track is to find body-cleansing substitutes for body-clogging foods and drinks.

Here are some common body-clogging foods and their body-cleansing substitutes. When you crave one of the following body-clogging foods, stop and ask yourself what is really motivating your hunger. If it is an emotional need, attend to it in a way that does not involve food (see some of the ideas for changing your eating habits on pages 11 to 13). If you are really physically hungry then remind yourself that food is a type of medicine and try the body-cleansing substitutes instead.

This list is just a starting point. There are many delicious recipes at the back of this book that will inspire you to consume more body-cleansing foods. You can also try your own variations using your favourite body-cleansing foods and you'll be surprised at just how many delicious food options are available to you.

It has taken you a lifetime to develop your present eating patterns so don't expect to change your tastes overnight. It will take a while to lose your cravings for certain foods, but it will happen if you persevere. The more good food you eat the more you will crave it. You will have more energy, you will look and feel better and your body will reward you for the goodness you have given it.

| BODY-CLOGGING FOOD | BODY-CLEANSING SUBSTITUTE |
| --- | --- |
| Hot chips | Homemade potato wedges lightly sprayed with cooking spray, sea salt and black pepper and baked in the oven on a non-stick tray until crisp |
| Soft drinks and alcohol | Fresh fruit frappé. Blend fresh fruit of your choice with cold water and ice cubes. Try strawberries, mangoes, pineapple and rockmelon (pineapple makes the drink lovely and creamy) |
| Cheese | Goat's cheese or sheep's cheese—there are some great varieties available |
| Gluten-containing foods, such as bread | Rice cakes, corn cakes, rice crackers, brown rice |
| Sweet biscuits, cakes and chocolate | Muffins made with fruit, fresh fruit, dried fruit and nuts |
| Chips, dips and savoury biscuits | Hummus or vegetable dips with vegetable sticks, plain unsalted nuts, rice crackers, popcorn (made with olive oil instead of butter), olives |
| Coffee and tea | Herbal teas, decaffeinated tea and coffee, hot water with lemon juice and honey |
| Red meat | Fish, free-range organic chicken |
| Sandwiches and pasta | Soup, salad, risotto, baked potatoes, baked vegetables |

# 3

# Exercise

# What are the benefits of exercise?

 After diet, exercise is the most important element of the 7 day health and vitality plan. The benefits of exercise could fill an entire book, however, those particularly relevant to the 7 day health and vitality plan are listed below.

Exercise will help:

- improve cardiovascular fitness
- improve circulation
- enhance lymphatic circulation
- improve the quality of your sleep
- increase energy
- speed up your metabolism
- relieve constipation
- enhance self-esteem
- lengthen life
- relieve depression and anxiety
- reduce alcohol consumption
- increase water consumption
- burn fat

These are just a few of the many benefits of exercise, but they will give you an idea of just how important it is to try to make the time to fit exercise into your life. The rewards you reap will far exceed the effort put into making time for exercise.

# How do you stay motivated?

Most people find exercise itself easy, but find it hard to stay motivated and put the time aside to do it. All you need is 30 minutes a day and if you put your mind to it you will find that it is surprisingly easy to incorporate exercise into your daily routine.

Instead of driving to the shops, why not walk? Get off your bus or train one stop earlier and walk the rest of the way to work. While you are watching TV, do some stretches, sit-ups and other exercises—or turn off the TV and go for a walk instead. There are countless ways that you can incorporate exercise into your day, and soon you will be doing 30 minutes or more without even thinking about it.

There are some easy ways to keep yourself motivated. You know what works best for you and what motivates you, so pick an idea from the list below and get going!

**Exercise with a friend**
You will push each other to train and exercising with someone else turns it into a social occasion, a chance to catch up. Exercising with a friend takes away the monotony of doing it by yourself and you will find the time will fly.

## Vary your routine

This will make exercise a lot more interesting than if you just do the same thing every day. It is also better for your body—you will get faster results from cross training.

## Do something that you enjoy

If you enjoy social contact and meeting new people, you will probably enjoy exercising as part of a team. But if you're looking for 'time out', yoga or individual circuit work may be what you need.

## Change your attitude

If you focus on the rewards and benefits of exercise rather than the effort needed to achieve them you will be more inclined to stick with a program. Look at the list on page 27 if you need a reminder of why exercise is so good for you.

## Set yourself goals and reward yourself

Rather than being overwhelmed by long-term goals, try setting weekly fitness goals that are achievable and giving yourself rewards for reaching them. Obviously don't use chocolate or alcohol as a reward or you will be defeating the purpose of exercising! What about a new book, a night out at the movies or a new accessory?

## Hire a personal trainer

If you can afford it, this is probably the best way to stay motivated and find the exercise program that is right for you. If you can't afford it by yourself, you and a friend could hire one together. Most gyms have in-house personal trainers, so if you belong to one make an appointment to see their personal trainer as often as you can.

## Stick at it

The more you exercise, the better you will feel and look. Once you get into a regular routine, you will find that you miss exercise if you don't do it and it soon becomes a pleasurable activity that you look forward to.

# What type of exercise should you do?

The best type of exercise is exercise that you enjoy. Many people do not enjoy gyms and aerobic classes and think that this means they don't like exercise. But there are many other types of exercise that suit different ages and lifestyles.

If you are young and single, why not join a sporting group? These are often organised at work places and are a great way to make new friends, and will keep you motivated because you are part of a team and are exercising with other people. And believe it or not, going to a nightclub and dancing the night away is a sensational workout!

If you are at home with young kids, one of the best ways to exercise is walking them in their prams. Young babies and children love to be out in the fresh air enjoying a change of scenery, and pushing them up hills in a pram certainly gives you a great workout! If your kids are older, take them down to the local park after school and kick a ball about or throw a Frisbee together. Go for bushwalks at the weekend, or go to the beach—walking on the sand is wonderful exercise.

As you get older, walking and swimming are great forms of exercise. Yoga and dancing are other alternatives. There are many clubs designed for older people's needs that incorporate some form of exercise.

## Do you need to cross train?

Cross training refers to a combination of different types of exercise. It is a good idea to try to vary your routine so that you do not become bored, and so that all parts of your body receive a workout.

Women, especially, should try to incorporate some form of weight-bearing exercise into their routines as this will help prevent osteoporosis. Good forms of weight-bearing exercise include walking, jogging, aerobics, skipping, weight training and dancing.

Another type of exercise is aerobic or cardiovascular. This type gives you more energy and strengthens your heart. It will raise your heart rate and you will feel as though you have had a thorough workout. Aerobic exercise includes brisk walking, running, jogging, tennis, skiing, cycling, surfing, rowing, dancing and squash.

Yoga is an excellent form of exercise for achieving and maintaining flexibility. It relaxes and tones your muscles, improves circulation and concentration, and can relieve emotional problems such as depression and stress.

# 4

# Caring for your body

Caring for your body includes having treatments such as massage, dry-skin brushing, exfoliation, water therapy, and improving your breathing and posture. You do not need a lot of time or money to have these treatments, because you can do them all by yourself at home. Caring for your body not only enhances your health and vitality, it makes you look and feel better, which is great for your self-esteem.

# Massage

As with exercise, the benefits of massage are numerous. Massage will:

- relieve stress
- increase lymphatic flow
- relax muscles
- tone the muscles
- improve the appearance of cellulite
- help the body eliminate excess fluids and waste products
- lower blood pressure
- increase blood circulation

**Self-massage**
It would be wonderful to have regular massages from a professional, but it is just not practical or affordable for most people. However, here are some simple self-massage techniques you can use at home to get the

benefits of massage on a daily basis. And if you have a partner, you can massage each other using these techniques.

This is not difficult to do; nor does it take much time. Just remember the following when you are massaging:

- All strokes should be towards the heart.
- Only massage when you are warm and relaxed.
- Start lightly and slowly, and gradually build to a firmer pace.
- Use the ends of your fingers or the flat of your palm.

It is impossible to cover all of your body every day—so just try to cover one small section each day, for example, face and neck or thigh and buttock. Here's how to do it:

- FACE AND NECK
  Use your fingertips and circle all over your face, working each part of it individually, then work down your neck in small and large circles.
- LOWER BACK AND SPINE
  Put your hands on your hips with the thumbs at your back. Firmly press your thumbs into your spine and lower back, moving in deep, firm circles.
- HAND AND WRIST
  Use the thumb of one hand to stroke the other from your knuckles to your wrist for each finger. Then swap hands.
- STOMACH AND CHEST
  Place your hands on your stomach and massage your torso in big circles, with the left hand going clockwise

and the right hand going anticlockwise.

- **THIGH AND BUTTOCK**
  Sit on the edge of the bed and work on one thigh at a time. With flat hands, massage the thigh area firmly, and once it is warm and pink continue with your fists.
- **SHOULDER AND ARM**
  Place your hand flat on your lower arm and massage the blood upwards, over your shoulder.
- **CALF AND FOOT**
  Brush your hands up from your feet to your knees in long, firm strokes.

# Dry-skin brushing

 Dry-skin brushing is an old natural healing method that increases both blood and lymphatic circulation. It also helps minimise the appearance of cellulite, allows the skin to 'breathe', softens the skin and rids the body of toxins. Stimulating the skin benefits all the other organs in the body as well, by improving circulation.

To dry-skin brush, use a natural-bristle dry-skin brush—you can buy these at health-food shops. Make your strokes short and brisk and directed towards the heart. Start with your arms (front and back) moving from the fingertips up into the armpit. Then repeat with the legs. Brush each leg up to the pelvis, and around to the lower back. Then do the chest and upper back, brushing towards the heart. You can also do the head and face, brushing downwards.

Always keep your brush dry and only dry-skin brush when your body is dry. Brush lightly at first and if it is painful just try to persevere. The discomfort will soon pass, and you will feel rejuvenated because of daily dry-skin brushing, and have glowing skin and smooth thighs.

# Exfoliation

Exfoliation is basically a wet version of dry-skin brushing. Instead of a bristle brush you use an exfoliant (either a cream or a gel) and water. Exfoliation has the same benefits as dry-skin brushing but has the added advantage of being relaxing, and it can be part of a bath ritual that involves aromatherapy oils. It is also gentler than dry-skin brushing so it can be used on the face. However, exfoliation takes a lot longer than dry-skin brushing, so it is not something you would do every day.

Exfoliation can be done once or twice a week as part of a relaxing 'time out' session in the privacy of your bathroom. An exfoliating scrub consists of two main ingredients: an abrasive (salt, sand or oats) that sloughs away the dead skin, and a moisturiser (oil, lotion or honey) that then moisturises the smooth skin. You can either buy special exfoliating scrubs or make one yourself. Simply add a teaspoon of salt, sand or rolled oats to your favourite bath oil or lotion.

To exfoliate, you basically give yourself a massage (see the section on self-massage on page 35), rubbing in the exfoliating scrub as you go. Get into a warm bath and soak your body. Get out and apply the scrub. When you have covered your entire body—paying particular attention to elbows, knees and feet—rub it off in the bath. Then dry yourself and apply a good moisturiser all over. You should be tingling all over and smell delicious.

# Water therapy

This is a very easy way of stimulating your circulatory and lymphatic systems, and toning your muscles and skin. Cold showers actually increase your circulation and warm you up, whereas lukewarm showers will cool you down more.

Have your hot shower as usual first thing in the morning. When you are ready to get out, turn off the hot tap and stand under the cold water for as long as you can, but preferably for at least one minute. If you have time, turn the hot tap back on again and then finish with another burst of cold water. Then dry yourself and quickly get dressed.

You will find that you feel totally invigorated by this therapy (once you get over the shock of it!) and you should feel squeaky-clean inside and out. It will certainly help you wake up in the morning. If you live near an ocean or lake or have a pool, you can also start your day with a brisk swim.

# Breathing and posture

When we are anxious our breathing becomes faster and more shallow; when we are relaxed we breathe more deeply and slowly. Deep breathing is important because it means that we inhale more oxygen so that there is more oxygen in our blood. Deep breathing also relaxes the mind and relieves stress.

Alternate-nostril breathing is a very simple exercise that will help you breathe to your full capacity. Sit in a comfortable position and slowly exhale all the air from your lungs. Close your right nostril by pressing with your thumb, and slowly and deeply inhale through your left nostril. When your lungs are full, remove your thumb from the right-hand nostril, press the left nostril closed and exhale through the right nostril. Repeat this several times, and keep practising until you can do up to 60 breaths.

Another good exercise is to practise deep breathing that fills your abdomen with air, instead of the shallower breathing that only fills your lungs. You can do this by placing your fingers over your stomach, and feeling it expand and deflate as you take in a deep breath and then exhale. Once you are proficient at both alternate-nostril breathing and deep breathing, you can do them together.

Posture is also important for body cleansing. If our posture is incorrect, our organs do not perform at their optimum, especially those used in the process of digestion. Sitting erect aids digestion by taking pressure off the abdomen and allowing air to move freely. Good posture also allows your lungs to expand more fully and therefore take in more oxygen. Regular exercise can help you maintain good posture.

# 5

# Looking
# after
# **yourself**

# The body as a whole

It is impossible to separate our emotional selves from our physical selves, as one simply does not exist without the other and each has a major impact on the other. As mentioned previously, eating is often motivated by emotional needs and stress can have a major impact on our physical health. And vice versa, when we are physically unwell, or even just unhealthy, we can often become depressed and lethargic.

Modern medicine is becoming more and more focused on the person as a whole, which is also why traditional forms of healing (that have always treated both the physical and the emotional self) are gaining in popularity. It is now widely accepted that we need to tend to our emotional and psychological needs, as well as addressing the physical issues in order to make long-term changes to our health.

While you are on the 7 day health and vitality plan, there are some very simple emotional and psychological exercises that will complement the physical aspects of the program. These exercises are easy to do, will not take a lot of time and they cost nothing. The benefits are numerous, and they include:

- boosting your self-esteem
- giving you a fresh outlook on life
- helping you deal with stress

- recharging your energy and zest for living
- freeing you from guilt
- letting go of old hatreds and grudges
- focusing your energies into constructive rather than destructive paths
- making you less reliant on others to meet your emotional needs
- making you a happier person, with more to give to others and yourself

# Positive thinking

Positive thinking is one of the simplest ways to change your whole outlook on life and how you feel about yourself and others. However, doing it is easier said than done, especially when you have been used to thinking in a negative way. To start thinking in a more positive way, you will need to practise changing your mindset. Here are some simple exercises to start you off.

**Turning negatives into positives**
When something goes wrong or annoys you, try to think of how you can turn it into a positive. For example, if your work computer crashes and you loose a document:

- You can take some time out from a busy day for a break.
- You have the opportunity to write an even better document once your computer is up and running again.
- Your boss might finally give you the new computer you've been asking for.

Worrying about the lost document will only stress you out and will not bring it back. Take a deep breath instead, and go for a walk while your computer is being fixed.

## Changing your attitude to others

There are probably some people you don't particularly like but you can't avoid, such as relatives, colleagues, neighbours, maybe even your flatmate. It can be very depressing to have to interact with people that you just can't seem to get along with and you may find that you start to dread situations where you have to see them.

The most important thing to remember is that you can't change other people or their behaviour. This means that the best way of dealing with these people is to change your attitude towards them. Try focusing on their positive qualities rather than their negative ones (everyone has some good points) and don't allow yourself to be drawn into an argument with them. If you change your attitude towards them you will find that their attitude towards you will change as well. People respond well to others who take an interest in them and like them.

Don't take other people's bad moods personally. Often the cause of someone's bad mood is something you know nothing about, yet you can take it on yourself and wonder what you have done to cause it. Never presume what is wrong and just give them some space. And, above all, don't let them make you feel bad. Work on your self-esteem, and remember you don't need to be liked by everybody in order to feel good about yourself! There are many books available that can help you deal with low self-esteem. Your local library or bookshop will probably have an entire section devoted to the topic. Choose an author you feel comfortable with and stick at it—it takes time.

## Conquering your fears

Fear can be paralysing, limiting people's lives in many ways. There are events that you may fear: exams, public speaking, meeting new people, etc. Just thinking about these can cause an outbreak of physical symptoms, such as nausea, sweating and shaking. But when you look closely at these dreaded occasions you will often find that it is your attitude to them rather than the event itself that is crippling you.

There are a few things you can practise to overcome these fears. First, think about what is the worst thing that can happen to you. It often isn't that bad. Second, conquer your fear by doing what you fear often, for example, join a toastmasters association if you are scared of public speaking. Third, remember that no one wants you to fail, especially at things such as public speaking. Everyone wants you to succeed.

## Cutting your mind chatter

People can be their own worst enemies with the negative self-talk they have constantly running through their heads. Have a listen to the voices in your head. Are you constantly undermining yourself by saying you're not good enough, slim enough, attractive enough, etc? This self-talk often starts in our childhood when we take on board criticisms from others, and then internalise these comments and start to believe in them ourselves. The easiest way to cut mind chatter is to play devil's advocate. Start telling yourself the opposite of what your mind is thinking. For example, if your mind is saying,

'I can't do it', tell yourself that you can and you will. Challenge your mind chatter by always asking yourself why you believe a particular thought.

# Relaxation and stress mangement

Learning to relax is a very valuable tool for stress management. We all need a little stress in our lives to excite, motivate and challenge ourselves, but too much stress can be overwhelming and eventually make us sick. Some people need a certain level of stress to function, while the same level of stress would shatter many others.

Achieving the right level of stress is often impossible, as there are so many factors out of our control. So, the best way to manage stress is to learn coping techniques that we can put in place when we find our stress levels are getting too high.

**Stressful situations**
When you are in a stressful situation, first try to take some time out. Even doing this for one minute can help you release some stress. While you are having your time out, remember to breathe deeply and slowly, as this will help control the physical symptoms of anxiety. If you can't remove yourself from the situation, you can still practise your breathing. And, finally, choose to remain calm. Tell yourself that you are going to remain in control of the situation by staying relaxed, cool and collected. It may sound simple, but it does work.

## Deep relaxation exercise

It is also helpful to practise some deep relaxation exercises you can do on a regular basis to relax and to revitalise yourself. If you practise these regularly, you will find that you will not get stressed as easily as before and that when you do get stressed you will cope better.

Try this exercise:

- Lie down in a quiet, dark room with some relaxing music.
- Slow your breathing down until it is deep, slow and feels natural.
- Visualise a happy, relaxing and secure place.
- Now visualise yourself in that place.
- Start with your feet; think about how relaxed they are. If you feel tense relax them.
- Continue this exercise, going all the way up your body until you have covered every part of it.
- Now take yourself back to the happy place and relax there for a while.
- When you are ready, take your mind back to your body and focus on how heavy and relaxed you feel.
- Slowly bring yourself back to consciousness, opening your eyes and then gradually getting up.
- Try to keep your calm feelings for as long as possible.

## Aromatherapy

Using aromatherapy oils is a very old and powerful form of healing. The oils work because our bodies inhale their molecules (either through the nose or the skin), and these then enter our bloodstream and travel to the brain to trigger certain functions. Never use more than the recommended quantity, as they can be dangerous if used incorrectly.

Aromatherapy oils can be used for massage, put into the bath, inhaled or placed in an oil burner.

- MASSAGE
  If you are using oils as a part of a massage, you will need to dilute them first (eight drops of essential oils to 20ml of base oil). The base oil should be a natural nut or seed oil. (See pages 35–37.)
- BATH
  Simply disperse a few drops of your chosen oil into the running water as you are filling the bath.
- INHALATION
  Place a few drops on a handkerchief (holding the cloth near your nose), or place a few drops in a basin of hot water, cover your head with a towel and place your face above the basin. Inhale the steam for about five minutes or until you have had enough.
- OIL BURNERS
  Fill the bowl of the burner with water, and then place a few drops of your oil into the water and light a candle underneath.

There are many different types of essential oils available, and your retailer will be able to advise you on the ones most suited to you. You may like to try rose, rosemary, geranium, juniper, eucalyptus, chamomile and lavender oils.

## Meditation

Meditation is one of the best ways to clear your mind. It releases tension, reduces stress levels, relaxes your body and slows down your 'internal chatter'. It also helps to improve your quality of sleep and will help you to remain calm in stressful situations. Meditation is a skill that you can continue to use long after you have finished your body-cleansing program.

The best way to learn meditation is to go to a class; however, if this is not an option try the following exercise.

- Go into a quiet, warm room where you will not be interrupted.
- Take the phone off the hook and put a 'do not disturb sign' on your front door.
- Get yourself into a comfortable position you will be able to stay in for at least 20 minutes.
- Choose a mantra, or chant, that you are able to say in a slow rhythm.
- Change your breathing so it is slow and deep.
- When you feel relaxed and calm, start to chant.
- When you are ready to stop, finish chanting and slowly change your breathing back to normal. Have a stretch and gradually get up to face the world.

Do not try to meditate for any more than 20 minutes at a time, but try to do it on a daily basis. You will be surprised at how quickly you get into the routine and at how beneficial it is to your whole outlook.

# 6

# Your
# 7 day
# health and
# vitality plan

# Preparing for health and vitality

 Although the 7 day health and vitality plan is a very safe procedure, there are some people who will not be able to do it. Do not commence this plan if you're:

- unwell or recovering from a cold or flu
- affected by chronic illness (especially one that involves the liver or kidneys; or diabetes or hypoglycaemia)
- pregnant or breast-feeding
- taking medication (check with your doctor to see if the 7 day health and vitality plan will interfere with its efficiency)
- dealing with high levels of stress at home or at work

Before beginning the plan, consult your doctor if you're unsure about any aspect of your health. Following your 7 day health and vitality plan will be a lot easier if you make some preparatory changes in the preceding week.

## Dietary preparation
The following are simple adjustments to your normal diet that start the process of self-cleansing. By making them you will help prepare your body for cleansing, and make it easier for yourself once you start the 7 day health and vitality plan.

- Cut down on caffeine consumption to one cup of tea or coffee per day.
- Reduce alcohol consumption to no more than one glass per day.
- Increase your water intake to eight glasses of bottled or filtered water per day.
- Eat at least two serves of vegetables per day.
- Eat at least two serves of fruit per day.

These simple changes are also great dietary guidelines to keep following once your detox is over. They form the basis of sensible, healthy living and will further extend the beneficial effects of the 7 day health and vitality plan.

## Mental preparation

Mental preparation is as important to the 7 day health and vitality plan as the physical preparation. Having the right mental attitude will totally change your whole perspective on detoxing and make the whole process pleasurable rather than painful.

The 7 day health and vitality plan is a process of looking after yourself and pampering your body—try to think of it as a treat, rather than as a chore. Don't think about the foods that you can't have, instead think of all the new foods you will be trying and the many ways in which you will be pampering your body—massage, meditation, etc.

Focus on how healthy you will be and how much energy you will have. If you adopt a positive attitude right from the start you will be more committed to the program and you will enjoy it more. You will also be more likely to incorporate the healthy changes you have made to your lifestyle after the 7 day health and vitality plan is over.

## Shopping list

Stocking up on the right equipment before you start the 7 day health and vitality plan will make the whole process much easier and less time-consuming.

BATHROOM

Now is a great time to indulge yourself by buying some of that beautiful aromatherapy oil you saw in a shop. By replacing food rewards with body care indulgences you will be able to nurture yourself in a way that is healthy, rewarding, and will make you look and smell fantastic.

Stock up on the following:

- a skin brush for dry-skin brushing
- an aromatherapy burner and oils
- a loofah and exfoliating creams
- moisturisers
- massage oils

KITCHEN

The kindest thing that you can do for yourself while detoxing is to remove the foods that are not on the detox list from your kitchen. If it's not there, you can't eat it. Stock your cupboards with a large range of foods from the detox list and ensure that you have plenty of healthy treats on hand for when the munchies strike.

If you have ever considered buying a juicer, now is a

great time to do it. You will also need:

- food containers for snacks (to carry with you and take to work)
- a steamer (the type you put over a wok or saucepan) for fish and vegetables
- olive oil
- honey
- fresh lemons
- vegetable juice (carrot or beetroot)
- garlic
- filtered or bottled water
- fresh food (see body-cleansing foods on page 16)

# The 7 day health and vitality plan

 Here's what you need to do while you are on the plan. You will find detailed descriptions of all these things earlier in the book; this list is just a summary of what you need to do.

**Every day**
- Start the day with a glass of hot water with lemon.
- Drink two litres of water.
- Eat at least four serves of vegetables and/or salad.
- Eat at least two serves of fruit.
- Eat one serve of rice.
- Eat as wide a variety of foods as possible.
- Have one serve of natural acidophilus yoghurt, cheese or milk (not made from cow's milk).
- Have two serves of pulses, nuts, fish or olive oil.
- Make sure you eat at least three meals.
- Exercise for at least 30 minutes.
- Have a 30-second cold shower every morning.
- Relax for at least ten minutes.
- Concentrate on posture and breathing.
- Dry-skin brush.

**Every second day**
- self-massage
- exfoliate

- do a relaxation exercise

**And finally**

While you are on the plan, do not consume:

- red meat
- cow's milk dairy products (except acidophilus yoghurt)
- chocolate
- gluten-containing grains
- sugar
- processed foods
- fast foods
- condiments such as salt and tomato sauce
- alcohol
- caffeine
- soft drinks
- fruit juice that has been sweetened

# Side effects of the 7 day health and vitality plan

After following the 7 day health and vitality plan you will feel wonderful. You will be recharged, revitalised and full of energy, sleeping deeply and soundly, and waking up feeling truly refreshed in the mornings. You will also look great and feel younger than you have in years.

However, depending on your state of health before you commenced the plan, you may experience a few side effects from it. These occur because your body is readjusting to your lifestyle changes and is purging itself of the toxins that have built up over the years.

Some of the side effects may include:

- headaches
- pimples, rashes and other skin problems
- tiredness
- furry tongue and bad breath
- constipation or loose bowel movements
- flatulence
- body odour and bad breath

Don't worry, these side effects won't last for long or be too severe. They are a good sign that your body is cleansing itself, and that you are well on the way to health and vitality.

# What happens when it's over?

Okay, so you've done the 7 day health and vitality plan and you're feeling fantastic. Where do you go from here? Well, first, don't undo all your good work. This doesn't mean that you must never touch a drop of alcohol or eat another chocolate again. What it does mean is that you should try to incorporate the basic principles of the plan into your everyday life. Some simple ways of doing this include exercising at least three times a week, avoiding caffeine, taking time out to relax on a regular basis and trying to drink eight glasses of water a day. Continue to base your diet on pure, unprocessed foods, and try to eat at least six serves a day of fruit and vegetables.

As well as using the plan as a guide for a healthier, happier life, you can use it as an opportunity to 'detox' when you feel yourself slipping back into bad habits or when you feel overloaded and overwhelmed. Just do it whenever you need to recharge and refocus.

As you can see, the 7 day health and vitality plan is about a lot more than just changing your eating habits and lifestyle for a week. Hopefully, it will motivate you to implement some lifelong changes to your physical and emotional health. The 7 day health and vitality plan should be your starting point for a happier, healthier and more vitalised you. Good luck!

# 7
# Eating
## your way to
# health
## and
# vitality

# Breakfast

# Wake-up citrus drink

 First thing in the morning, drink this hot wake-up beverage from your coffee mug or tea cup. It should be drunk on an empty stomach, because the acid in the fruit stimulates and 'wakes up' the gallbladder and digestive systems, preventing constipation. Citrus fruit is a great source of vitamin C and dietary fibre.

Juice from 1 lemon
Juice from ½ grapefruit
½ cup hot water
½ teaspoon raw honey

Pour lemon juice and grapefruit juice into a heatproof cup. Mix in hot water and honey with a fork. Drink immediately. Serves 1.

# Super banana smoothie

 We all know that breakfast is the most important meal of the day as it kick-starts the metabolism into action. This filling smoothie is high in calcium, fibre and protein.

1 cup soy milk
2 tablespoons natural acidophilus yoghurt
1 teaspoon raw honey
1 banana, peeled and chopped
2 heaped tablespoons rice bran or other gluten-
   free bran

Combine milk, yoghurt, honey, banana and rice bran in a blender. Blend for 1 minute or until smooth.

Pour the smoothie into a chilled glass. Drink immediately. Serves 1.

# Apple and beetroot detox drink

This healthy juice is a terrific way to start the day. Beetroot is often used to stimulate liver activity and relieve constipation. Because beetroot can have such a strong effect on the body it is diluted with apple, pear and celery. Apples and pears provide soluble fibre, while celery is a natural diuretic that helps to flush toxins from the body.

2 baby beetroot (about 100g) chopped
1 small apple, cored and quartered
1 ripe pear, cored and quartered
1 stick celery, chopped

In a juice extractor, first process the beetroot, then the apple, pear and celery. Stir well. Drink immediately. Serves 1.

# Super stress reliever

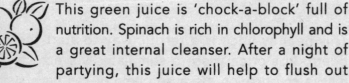 This green juice is 'chock-a-block' full of nutrition. Spinach is rich in chlorophyll and is a great internal cleanser. After a night of partying, this juice will help to flush out toxins and replenish your stressed system. Parsley and celery are natural diuretics that reduce excess body fluid, and grapes provide sweetness and potassium.

> 5 small spinach leaves, well washed
> 1 tablespoon parsley
> 1 stick celery, chopped
> 6 seedless green grapes

In a juice extractor, first process the spinach, then the parsley, celery and grapes. Stir well. Drink immediately. Serves 1.

# Rice porridge with mixed dried fruit

The 7 day health and vitality plan demands that you do not indulge in your favourite morning bowl of hot, steamy porridge. But there is an alternative—rice porridge from your local supermarket or health food store. You can add your own selection of dried fruit or use my suggestions. This delicious, hearty porridge is gluten free, high in complex carbohydrates, and low in fat and salt.

    1 cup rice porridge
    2½ cups water
    ½ teaspoon cinnamon
    Optional: 1 teaspoon each—sultanas, diced dried
        apple, finely chopped dried apricots
    2 teaspoons raw honey
    1 cup soy milk

Combine the rice porridge, water, cinnamon and dried fruit in a medium saucepan. Bring to the boil over a medium-high heat, stirring constantly. Boil for 2 minutes. Remove from the heat and stir. Allow to stand for 1 minute.

To serve, spoon the porridge into two serving bowls, then drizzle honey on top and pour soy milk over. Serve immediately. Serves 2.

# Scrambled tofu with mushrooms

 This dish almost looks and tastes like scrambled eggs—the eggs being replaced with tofu. Adding grated carrot and fried onion binds the mixture and enhances the taste and appearance. Tofu is a great source of protein and phytoestrogens (plant-based oestrogen), while carrots and mushrooms add vitamin A, folic acid, vitamin B2 and B3, potassium and fibre.

2 teaspoons olive oil
½ onion, finely diced
1 small carrot, peeled and grated
2 small white mushroom caps, thinly sliced
250g firm tofu, crumbled
2 teaspoons salt-reduced soy sauce
4 rice cakes

In a large non-stick frying pan, heat 1 teaspoon oil over medium-high heat, and sauté onions and carrot for about 3 minutes or until golden brown. Add mushrooms and sauté for 1 minute. Remove onion mixture and set aside.

Add remaining 1 teaspoon of oil and sauté tofu, mashing well for about 3 minutes or until golden brown. Add onion mixture and sauté for 1 minute. Stir in soy sauce and serve immediately with rice cakes. Serves 2.

# Compote of fruit with yoghurt

You can eat this dish for breakfast, lunch or dinner, depending on your appetite at the time. Apple juice is used instead of sugar for sweetening. Rhubarb is a great source of fibre, potassium, vitamin C and manganese.

2 cups apple juice with no added sugar
3 strips orange rind
1 stick cinnamon
500g rhubarb, cut into 12mm pieces
2 apples, peeled and cut into 8 pieces
2 ripe pears, peeled and cut into 8 pieces
½ cup plain acidophilus yoghurt for serving

In a saucepan, heat apple juice, orange rind and cinnamon stick over medium heat for 1 minute. Add rhubarb, apple and pear. Cover the saucepan with a tight-fitting lid and bring to the boil. Lower heat to simmer and cook for about 10 minutes or until fruit is just cooked. Remove from heat and leave for about 10 minutes. Cool and serve with yoghurt. Serves 2–4.

# Citrus fruit salad

Oranges, grapefruit, mandarins, limes, lemons, tangelos and pomelos are all members of the citrus fruit family. When buying citrus fruit, make sure that it is plump and heavy for its size; fruit with a lot of pith and rind is usually dry and old. These fruits are available all year, and are excellent sources of vitamin C and dietary fibre. Enjoy this quick and easy salad with a little raw honey (available from health-food shops).

 2 navel oranges, peeled and diced
 1 pink grapefruit, peeled and diced
 1 mandarin, peeled and diced
 1 teaspoon raw honey

In a large bowl, combine oranges, grapefruit, mandarin and honey. Stir well and set aside for 15 minutes. Serve in glass bowls. Serves 2.

# Lunch

# Watercress and spinach soup

This soup relies on yoghurt and lemon juice to bring out its natural sharpness. It has a strong sour taste and a fantastic green colour. Watercress is used as a natural detoxifier and internal cleanser. Spinach contains glutathione, which aids detoxification.

1 teaspoon olive oil
2 bunches (about 250g) watercress, stems
    removed, rinsed, dried and shredded
500g baby spinach, stems removed, rinsed, dried
and shredded
1½ tablespoons fresh lemon juice
350ml natural acidophilus yoghurt
½ teaspoon freshly ground pepper
Natural acidophilus yoghurt for serving

In a large saucepan or soup pot, heat oil over medium heat, and cook watercress and spinach for about 1 minute. Lower heat and cover saucepan with a tight-fitting lid, and cook for about 10 minutes or until watercress mixture has softened. Turn off heat and leave for 5 minutes.

Transfer mixture to a blender or food processor, and blend until smooth; stopping and scraping down sides of container as needed. Add lemon juice, yoghurt and pepper, and blend until the mixture is smooth.

Return soup to saucepan and reheat for 3 minutes.

Ladle soup into individual bowls, garnish with a drop of yoghurt and serve at once. Serves 4–6.

# Cannellini bean and cabbage soup

 This authentic Italian dish is an economical one and can be prepared in summer using fresh tomatoes or in winter using the tinned variety. Cabbage is a great detoxification food and is a great source of fibre and vitamin C. Cannellini beans are a great source of fibre and complex carbohydrates.

2 teaspoons olive oil
1 medium onion, finely diced
3 cloves garlic, crushed
1 cup chopped celery leaves
4 sticks celery, chopped
½ cup chopped parsley
1 medium carrot, grated
2 large vine-ripened tomatoes, diced
3 tablespoons tomato paste
6 black peppercorns, crushed
4 cups vegetable stock
4 cups finely shredded cabbage
1x240g tin cannellini (white beans), well rinsed
1 tablespoon chopped parsley for serving

Over medium heat in a large saucepan or stockpot, heat oil and sauté onion for about 5 minutes or until softened but not brown. Add garlic and sauté for 1 minute. Add celery leaves, chopped celery, parsley, carrot, tomatoes, tomato paste, peppercorns and vegetable stock. Bring to the boil, then reduce heat and simmer for about 20 minutes or until vegetables are tender, stirring occasionally. Stir in cabbage and cannellini beans, and cook for 15 minutes or until cabbage is cooked.

Ladle the hot soup into bowls, garnish with parsley and serve. Serves 4–6.

# Spicy kohlrabi and sweet potato soup

Kohlrabi, meaning 'cabbage turnip', is a misunderstood vegetable—it suffers from an identity crisis. As a member of the cabbage (brassica) family, it grows above the ground and is not a root vegetable, as is commonly thought. It has a similar flavour to turnip and can be substituted for it in recipes. Two main types are grown—white and purple. It contains a lot of water and does not store well.

2 teaspoons olive oil
1 cup thinly sliced leeks, including some light
    green section
1 onion, diced
250g butternut pumpkin, peeled seeded and cut
    into 2cm cubes
250g sweet potato, peeled and diced
2 kohlrabi, washed, peeled and cut into 2cm cubes
4 cups vegetable or chicken stock
¼ teaspoon cayenne pepper
½ teaspoon pepper
2 tablespoons chopped parsley

Over low heat in a heavy saucepan, heat the oil, and sauté leeks and onion for about 5 minutes or until tender. Add pumpkin, sweet potato, kohlrabi, chicken stock, cayenne pepper and pepper. Cover and bring to the boil, then reduce heat and simmer uncovered for about 30 minutes or until vegetables are very soft.

Puree mixture in a blender or food processor. Remove soup to saucepan and reheat for 5 minutes.

Ladle soup into individual bowls, garnish with parsley and serve at once. Serves 4.

# Kohlrabi and carrot salad

 Eaten raw, kohlrabi has a sweet turnip-like flavour. Weight for weight, they have more vitamin C than oranges. Kohlrabi can be boiled and pureed or eaten raw in a salad. Carrots are a great source of vitamin A and fibre.

2 medium kohlrabi, peeled and grated
1 tablespoon fresh lemon juice
2 medium carrots, grated
1 red-skinned apple, washed and grated
2 shallots, thinly sliced
2 tablespoons olive oil
2 tablespoons fresh orange juice
1 teaspoon grated fresh ginger
½ teaspoon pepper

In a large bowl, toss kohlrabi with lemon juice. Add carrots, apple and shallots and toss well.

In a screw-top jar, mix olive oil, orange juice, ginger and pepper until well combined. Pour dressing over salad and mix well. Let the salad stand at room temperature for 30 minutes before serving. Serves 2–4.

# Eggplant pizza

 This pizza can be eaten for lunch or dinner. On the 7 day health and vitality plan you are not allowed to eat most breads or cheeses— this delicious pizza uses neither, but relies on the fresh flavours of tomato, garlic and basil. When buying eggplants look for smooth, firm, shiny vegetables with no blemishes and avoid large ones, as they can be spongy with little taste.

3 teaspoons olive oil
1 medium onion, finely diced
2 cloves garlic, crushed
½ small red chilli, finely chopped
4 vine-ripened tomatoes, finely chopped
12 basil leaves, chopped
1 teaspoon fresh lemon juice
1 large eggplant, cut into 12 round slices
2 tablespoons chopped parsley

To make sauce, in a medium saucepan, heat 1 teaspoon of oil and sauté onion for about 3 minutes or until golden. Add garlic and chilli, and sauté for 1 minute. Add tomatoes, basil and lemon juice. Bring to the boil, stirring constantly. Reduce heat and simmer for 10 minutes.

Heat 1 teaspoon of oil in a large non-stick frying pan

and cook half the eggplant slices for about 8–10 minutes or until light brown, turning once during cooking. Heat the remaining 1 teaspoon of oil and cook the remaining eggplant slices. Keep cooked eggplant warm.

Place spoonfuls of tomato sauce on top of eggplant slices, garnish with parsley and serve immediately. Serves 2–3.

# Beetroot and basil salad

Beetroot is available all year but is best and freshest from July to November. Choose beetroot that is smooth, firm and a good colour. Beetroot has one of the highest sugar contents of any vegetable, and is a good source of most minerals (including potassium), iron and dietary fibre.

4 baby beetroot (about 200g), washed, scrubbed
    and grated
12 basil leaves, chopped
4 cups mixed lettuce leaves, washed and dried
¼ teaspoon pepper
2 teaspoons olive oil
2 teaspoons lemon juice

Toss beetroot and basil together.

In a large bowl, place lettuce on the bottom then top it with beetroot and basil mixture. Season with pepper.

Just before serving, drizzle olive oil and lemon juice over salad and toss well. Serves 2–4.

# Warm beetroot and spinach with horseradish cream

This colourful salad is full of antioxidants vitamins A and C, iron and fibre. Beetroot cleanses the blood, and increases kidney and liver activity. As the active nutrients in the beetroot flush out your kidneys, you will notice a distinct pink colour in your urine and faeces; do not be concerned.

4 baby beetroot, washed and scrubbed
1 teaspoon olive oil
1 teaspoon balsamic vinegar
1 teaspoon natural acidophilus yoghurt
½ teaspoon horseradish
½ teaspoon pepper
4 cups English spinach, washed and deribbed

Preheat oven to 190°C. Pierce beetroot several times with a skewer and wrap each one in a sheet of aluminium foil. Bake for 1–1½ hours or until tender, when a skewer is inserted. Allow the beetroot to cool enough to handle and peel away the skin. Dice the beetroot.

In a screw-top jar, combine olive oil, vinegar, horseradish and pepper, and shake well. In a bowl, toss beetroot with dressing.

Place spinach and beetroot mixture in a large salad bowl and toss well. Serve immediately. Serves 2–4.

# Traditional Italian salad

There are many different varieties of lettuce available today—cos, radicchio, rocket, endive, butter and oakleaf are just a few. Lettuce is an excellent source of dietary fibre and a good source of potassium. Experiment with different varieties of lettuce to find new ones that you like.

4 cups assorted lettuce leaves, washed and torn apart
2 vine-ripened tomatoes, cut into 8 wedges
12 fresh basil leaves, torn apart
12 black olives, pitted and halved
2 tablespoons finely diced red (Spanish) onion
½ ripe avocado, diced
½ teaspoon freshly ground pepper
2 tablespoons balsamic vinegar
2 teaspoons olive oil

In a large bowl, toss lettuce leaves, tomatoes, basil leaves, olives, onion and avocado together. Season with pepper.

Just before serving, drizzle vinegar and oil over the salad and toss well. Serves 2.

# Colourful coleslaw

In this colourful salad, red and green cabbage is used to give a vivid visual effect. Cabbage is one of the top detox foods and is an excellent source of vitamin C when raw (more than half is usually lost in the cooking water when it is boiled).

SALAD
4 cups finely shredded green cabbage
4 cups finely shredded red cabbage
2 medium carrots, grated
1 unpeeled red apple, grated
2 Lebanese cucumbers, washed and diced
2 shallots, finely sliced
2 tablespoons flat-leaf (Italian) parsley

DRESSING
$\frac{1}{3}$ cup fresh lime or lemon juice
2 teaspoons olive oil
1 teaspoon Dijon mustard
1 clove garlic, crushed
$\frac{1}{2}$ teaspoon freshly ground pepper

In a large bowl, combine green cabbage, red cabbage, carrots, apple, cucumbers, shallots and parsley. Mix very well.

In a small screw-top jar, combine lime or lemon juice,

oil, Dijon mustard, garlic and pepper, and shake until blended. Pour dressing over salad and toss well. Cover and refrigerate for up to 3 hours. Serves 4–6.

# Green rice salad

Capsicum is a good source of vitamins A and C. For added nutritional value you can also add shredded fresh spinach to the salad. This salad can be made with any leftover hot plain rice. This dish is best eaten at room temperature as the flavours are at their peak. If there is any rice salad left over, cover and refrigerate for up to 2 days.

DRESSING
2 teaspoons Dijon mustard
4 tablespoons fresh lemon juice
1/4 cup olive oil
2 teaspoons raw honey
1/2 teaspoon freshly ground pepper

SALAD
5 cups hot, cooked rice
1 cup cooked green peas
1/2 green capsicum, seeded, deribbed and diced
2 shallots, finely diced
1 tablespoon chopped fresh mint
1 tablespoon chopped fresh parsley
1 tablespoon chopped fresh basil
1 cup cooked chick peas, well drained

In a screw-top jar, combine dressing ingredients and shake well.

Pour the dressing over hot rice and mix well. Add peas, capsicum, shallots, mint, parsley, basil and chickpeas, and mix well. Cover salad until serving time. Serves 4–6.

# Light Waldorf salad

Waldorf salad is traditionally made with lots of mayonnaise for richness. This light alternative uses the creaminess of yoghurt which adds a delicious tartness. This salad is best served immediately after making to preserve the crispness of the apples and celery.

3 unpeeled red apples, cored and diced
3 tablespoons fresh orange juice
2 sticks celery, thinly sliced
½ cup sultanas
½ cup chopped walnuts
4 tablespoons natural acidophilus yoghurt

In a large bowl, mix together apple and orange juice. Add celery, sultanas, walnuts and yoghurt and mix well. Serve immediately. Serves 2–4.

# Watercress and mushroom salad

Watercress is a member of the cruciferous, or bassica, family known for its detox and cancer-fighting qualities. Watercress should have dark-green fresh-looking leaves that are crisp, tender and free from dirt. Enjoy this lunchtime salad with a rice cracker and hummus (see page 134). The salad contains excellent sources of dietary fibre, vitamin A, vitamin C and vitamin E.

SALAD
1 small bunch watercress, washed and dried
1 red delicious apple, cored and thinly sliced
4 small white mushrooms, thinly sliced
2 tablespoons lemon juice
1/4 cup raw cashew nuts, chopped
2 shallots, thinly sliced

DRESSING
1/2 ripe avocado, mashed
2 tablespoons lemon juice
1 tablespoon orange juice
1 teaspoon Balsamic vinegar
Few drops Tabasco

Remove any yellow leaves from watercress. Tear stems into bite-sized pieces.

In a large salad bowl, mix watercress, apple, mushrooms, 2 tablespoons of lemon juice, cashew nuts and shallots together.

In a small bowl, mix avocado, lemon juice, orange juice, vinegar and Tabasco together. Just before serving, mix dressing into salad. Serve immediately. Serves 2–4.

# Persian-flavoured rice

When you have time to cook yourself a hot lunch, try this interesting Persian rice dish. Use any dried fruit you have in the cupboard to add variety and interest to this dish. Dried fruit is a great source of dietary fibre, iron, potassium and sweetness. Brown rice should be cooked and used throughout the 7 day health and vitality plan, as it is an excellent source of dietary fibre, vitamins and minerals.

1 teaspoon olive oil
1 onion, finely diced
2 cloves garlic, crushed
1½ teaspoons ground cumin
¾ teaspoon chilli powder
¾ teaspoon ground cinnamon
1 medium carrot, grated
1 medium zucchini, grated
¼ cup currants
¼ cup diced dried apricots
¼ cup chopped raw almonds
4 cups cooked brown rice
1–2 tablespoons lemon juice
½ cup chopped fresh coriander

Heat olive oil in a large non-stick frying pan and sauté onion for 5 minutes or until golden brown. Add garlic and sauté for 30 seconds. Add cumin, chilli powder and cinnamon, and sauté for 1 minute. Add carrot and zucchini flesh and cook for 1–2 minutes or until soft. Add currants, apricots, almonds and rice, and stir constantly for 1 minute. Mix in 1 tablespoon of lemon juice and taste. Add more lemon juice as needed. Garnish with coriander and serve immediately. Serves 2.

# Ratatouille

 This wonderful Mediterranean vegetable dish is jam-packed with nutrition. Almost any vegetable can be added to give ratatouille your own personal touch. The traditional version is made with onions, garlic, tomatoes, eggplant, capsicum and zucchini. All these vegetables are excellent sources of dietary fibre, as well as most vitamins and minerals. Ratatouille can be served either hot or cold with hot cooked rice.

2 teaspoons olive oil
1 medium onion, finely diced
3 cloves garlic, crushed
½ red capsicum, seeded, deribbed and diced
½ green capsicum, seeded, deribbed and diced
1 small eggplant, diced
3 zucchini, diced
3 vine-ripened tomatoes, diced
1 teaspoon dried basil
1 teaspoon dried oregano
½ teaspoon pepper
4 cups hot cooked brown rice

In a large non-stick saucepan, heat oil and sauté onion for 5 minutes or until it is golden brown. Add garlic and sauté for 30 seconds. Add red and green capsicum, eggplant, zucchini, tomatoes, basil, oregano and pepper. Stir well, cover and simmer for 20–30 minutes or until vegetables are soft. Serve hot with hot brown rice. Serves 4.

# Dinner

# Thai rice noodle soup

This delicious soup is made with authentic Thai ingredients. They can be purchased at Asian supermarkets or in the Asian section of most large supermarkets. Rice stick noodles are flat and the length of a chopstick. They are very easy to use, and combine well with tofu and mushrooms. Tamari can be purchased in health-food stores.

125g rice stick noodles
4 cups water
2 stalks lemon grass, cut into 3cm lengths
5 slices galangal
3 French shallots, peeled and chopped
2 small red chillies, cut in half
4 kaffir lime leaves
100g firm tofu, cut into 1cm cubes
12 shitake mushrooms, torn in half
12 white mushrooms, cut in half
4 tablespoons fresh lime juice
1 cup coriander leaves
3 tablespoons tamari

Cover rice stick with hot water and soak for about 10 minutes or until they are very soft. Drain well in a colander. Set aside.

In a medium saucepan, bring water, galangal,

shallots, chillies and kaffir lime leaves to the boil over high heat, stirring continuously. Reduce heat to medium, and add tofu and mushrooms—DO NOT STIR. Cover saucepan with a tight-fitting lid and cook for 3 minutes. Stir in rice stick noodles. Turn off heat and stir in lime juice, coriander leaves and tamari. Serve immediately. Serves 3–4.

# Spicy red lentil and vegetable soup

This hearty, nutritious soup makes a substantial dinner. It can be made during the day and reheated. Red lentils belong to the pulse and lentil family. They are a great source of protein and fibre, and have been known to lower blood cholesterol. Pulses contain soluble and insoluble forms of fibre. Insoluble fibre promotes regular bowel movements, and so helps to guard against constipation.

¾ cup dried red lentils
2 teaspoons olive oil
1 onion, finely chopped
3 cloves garlic, crushed
4 cups vegetable stock
2 sticks celery, chopped
2 medium carrots, peeled and diced
1 bay leaf
3 vine-ripened tomatoes, chopped
½ teaspoon cayenne pepper
½ teaspoon pepper
2 tablespoons chopped parsley

Rinse lentils in a colander. Soak them in very hot water for 10 minutes. Drain well in a colander.

In a large saucepan, over medium heat, heat oil and sauté onions for 3 minutes. Add garlic and sauté for 30 seconds. Add lentils, vegetable stock, celery, carrots, bay leaf, tomatoes, cayenne pepper and pepper. Cover and bring to the boil, then skim the scum off the surface of the soup. Reduce heat and simmer uncovered for about 45 minutes or until lentils are very soft. Stir frequently so that lentils do not stick to the bottom. Remove bay leaf.

Ladle soup into individual bowls, garnish with parsley and serve. Serves 4–6.

# Vegetable and rice pasta with tomato and fennel sauce

 As there is no wheat-based pasta allowed in the 7 day health and vitality plan, this pasta is a great substitute. It is made with brown rice, spinach, beetroot and carrot and is gluten-free. Accompanied by the tasty tomato and fennel sauce, the pasta makes an ideal dinner when you are hungry. The vegetable and rice pasta can be purchased at health-food stores.

- 1 teaspoon olive oil
- 1 medium onion, finely diced
- 3 cloves garlic, crushed
- 1 small red chilli, seeds removed and finely chopped
- 1 teaspoon fennel seeds
- 12 basil leaves, chopped
- 2 medium carrots, peeled and grated on a box grater
- 1 stick celery, diced
- 2x240g tinned tomatoes in tomato juice, chopped
- 1x250g vegetable and rice pasta

To make sauce, in a medium saucepan, heat oil and sauté onion for about 3 minutes or until golden brown.

Add garlic, chilli, fennel seeds and basil leaves, and sauté for 1 minute. Add carrots and celery and sauté for 1 minute. Add chopped tomatoes and tomato juice, and bring to the boil, stirring constantly. Reduce heat and simmer for 30–40 minutes, stirring occasionally.

To cook pasta, in a large saucepan of boiling water, cook pasta for 8–10 minutes or until tender. Drain well. Mix sauce through pasta and serve immediately. Serves 3–4.

# Stir-fried rice noodles with vegetables

This is a warm, satisfying dish that is full of taste and nutrition. Rice noodles can be purchased from Asian markets or the Asian section of large supermarkets, and stored in your grocery cupboard. There are many different kinds of dry rice noodles, vermicelli and rice stick noodles available. The thicker the noodle the longer it should be soaked before using.

250g dry rice noodles
2 tablespoons tamari
2 tablespoons tomato paste
½ cup chicken or vegetable stock
1 teaspoon olive oil
2 cloves garlic, crushed
1x2cm piece ginger, grated
4 shallots, finely sliced
2 cups fresh bean sprouts
½ green capsicum, deribbed and cut into
    julienne strips
1/2 cup tinned water chestnuts, rinsed and
    thinly sliced
150g firm tofu, cut into 1cm cubes

Cover rice noodles with hot water for about 10 minutes

or until they are very soft. Drain well in a colander. Set aside.

In a small bowl, mix tamari, tomato paste and chicken stock together.

Heat oil in a wok or a large frying pan, and stir-fry garlic, ginger and shallots for 10 seconds. Add bean sprouts, capsicum, water chestnuts and tofu, and stir-fry for 3 minutes. Add noodles and sauce, and stir-fry for about 2 minutes or until heated through. Serve immediately. Serves 2–3.

# Vietnamese rice paper rolls

This dish relies on fresh ingredients and being eaten immediately after it has been made for optimum taste. You can prepare all the fillings, and then let your family or guests create their own rice paper rolls. Use a large variety of vegetables (steamed and raw) and shredded chicken or cooked tuna or salmon for variety.

1 small carrot, peeled and cut into julienne strips
1 small Lebanese cucumber, cut into julienne strips
2 shallots, cut into julienne strips
50g rice vermicelli noodles, soaked in hot water for
    10 minutes and well drained
½ cup chopped fresh mint
½ cup chopped coriander
½ cup bean sprouts
2 teaspoons tamari

DIPPING SAUCE
1 small red chilli, seeds removed and finely chopped
3 tablespoons water
1 tablespoon tamari
1 teaspoon honey
2 teaspoons chopped coriander
8 small to medium rice paper rounds

In a small bowl, mix chilli, water, tamari and honey together. Let mixture cool and add 2 teaspoons of coriander.

In a large bowl, mix carrot, cucumber, shallots, noodles, mint, coriander, bean sprouts and tamari together.

In a large bowl of cold water, soak rice paper rounds individually for about 3 minutes or until they are soft. Remove rice paper rounds carefully from the water and shake off as much excess water as possible. Lay rice paper rounds flat on a plate. Place one portion of the filling into the centre of the rice paper and roll up firmly, tucking in the sides. Repeat this process until all rice papers and filling are used. Serve immediately with dipping sauce. Serves 4.

# Vegetarian cabbage rolls

Cabbage is one of the top detox foods. It is cheap and plentiful all year round, and can be used either raw or cooked. This dish takes a little more time to prepare than most of the ones in this book but it is well worth the effort. Prepare and cook it the day before you intend to eat it, or when you have some spare time, and reheat it in your microwave.

8 large cabbage leaves
2 teaspoons olive oil
1 onion, finely chopped
4 cloves garlic, crushed
2 carrots, peeled and grated
2 zucchini, grated
8 white mushrooms, coarsely chopped
1 cup cooked long-grain rice
½ teaspoon paprika
¼–½ teaspoon cayenne pepper
2 tablespoons chopped parsley
½ teaspoon pepper
4 cups shredded cabbage
470g tin peeled tomatoes, drained (juice reserved) and chopped
1 cup water or vegetable stock
3 tablespoons tomato paste

Preheat oven to 180°C. Blanch cabbage leaves in boiling water for 2–3 minutes. Drain well, cut out hard middle core and set leaves aside.

Heat oil in a large non-stick frying pan over medium-high heat and sauté onion for about 5 minutes until golden brown. Add garlic and sauté for 1 minute. Add carrots, zucchini and mushrooms, and sauté for 3 minutes. Remove pan from heat, and mix in rice, paprika, cayenne pepper, parsley and pepper.

Divide rice mixture evenly into 8 portions and place 1 portion in centre of each cabbage leaf. Roll each one up carefully and tuck sides in firmly.

Spray a large casserole dish with olive oil cooking spray. Layer half of shredded cabbage on bottom and cover with a layer of 4 cabbage rolls placed seam-side down. Repeat with remaining cabbage and rolls.

Mix tomatoes, juice, water and tomato paste together, and pour over rolls. Cover with a lid or aluminium foil, and bake for about 1–1½ hours or until rolls are tender. Transfer rolls to serving plates, and spoon out the shredded cabbage and sauce. Serves 4.

# Barbecued salmon on potato mash with asparagus

Here is a meal fit for a king or a queen. It contains very little added oil but tastes rich and delicious. Salmon is an excellent source of Omega-3 fatty acids, while potato contains fibre, potassium and useful amounts of vitamin C.

4x200g Atlantic salmon fillets, with skin on
3 teaspoons olive oil
6 medium mashing potatoes, peeled and
    roughly chopped
½ teaspoon pepper
½ teaspoon garlic powder
16 sticks asparagus

Place salmon fillets in a shallow glass dish. Cover salmon with 1 teaspoon of olive oil.

Light a charcoal grill or preheat a gas grill. Spray the cooking rack with olive oil cooking spray.

In a large pot of boiling water, cook potatoes for about 10–12 minutes until they are just tender and cooked. Pour out excess water from potatoes. Vigorously mash them with a potato masher. Mix in pepper, garlic powder and remaining 2 teaspoons of olive oil. Cover and set aside in a warm spot.

When the grill is ready, place salmon on grill and cook for 3 minutes per side (rare) or 4 minutes per side (medium). While the salmon is cooking, prepare the asparagus. Steam asparagus for about 3–5 minutes or until just tender.

Place 1 portion of garlic mash onto each plate, top with cooked salmon. Serve asparagus on the side. Serve immediately. Serves 4.

# Ocean trout parcels with parsley potatoes

Ocean trout is a deep sea fish and can be used in recipes where salmon is called for, as it tastes very similar. It is usually less expensive than salmon but the fillets have more bones in them. Cooking fish in aluminium parcels preserves all the flavour and nutrition, and no oil is required. Baby potatoes are easy and quick to boil, and provide excellent fibre, potassium and complex carbohydrates.

4 boneless, skinless ocean trout fillets
4 teaspoons lemon juice
2 shallots, finely sliced
1 small carrot, peeled and grated
1 zucchini, grated
2 teaspoons chopped dill
Pepper to taste
Sprigs of dill and lemon wedges for serving
16 baby potatoes, scrubbed clean
2 tablespoons chopped parsley
2 teaspoons olive oil

Light a charcoal grill or preheat a gas grill. Spray the cooking rack with olive oil cooking spray.

In a large pot of boiling water, cook potatoes for

10 minutes or until they are tender and cooked through. Drain out all water. Mix parsley and oil into potatoes. Cover with a lid until fish is ready.

Tear 4 large square sheets of aluminium foil and spray them very lightly with olive oil cooking spray. Place a fillet of fish on each sheet and sprinkle each one with 1 teaspoon of lemon juice. Divide the shallots, carrot, zucchini and dill into 4 portions, and place 1 portion on top of each fillet of fish. Grind pepper onto each fillet. Fold the aluminium foil over to completely seal the parcel. Place parcels on the grill and cook for about 8 minutes or until cooked. Garnish with sprigs of dill and lemon wedges. Serve immediately with parsley potatoes. Serves 4.

# Fennel and tuna vinaigrette

 Fennel is sometimes called 'anise' because it has a mild anise, or liquorice, flavour. It is available from March to September and can be eaten raw or cooked. In India, roasted fennel seeds are chewed after eating to prevent bad breath and to aid digestion. In ancient Greece and Rome, the seeds were eaten to prevent obesity. Fennel is low in kilojoules and provides vitamin A, vitamin C, calcium, potassium and nitrates. Tuna is an excellent source of Omega-3 fatty acids.

2 small to medium fennel bulbs
3 tablespoons lemon juice
1 clove garlic, crushed
1 teaspoon dried oregano
1 tablespoon olive oil
½ teaspoon pepper
2 vine-ripened tomatoes, diced
1x180g tin tuna in olive oil or brine, drained
    and flaked
2 tablespoons chopped parsley

Cut off the tops of the fennel bulbs and trim the base. Pull off and discard all outer large, tough leaves. Cut each bulb into quarters lengthwise and cut out the core.

Finely shred the fennel.

In a large bowl, mix the shredded fennel and 2 tablespoons of lemon juice together.

In another bowl, mix garlic, oregano, 1 tablespoon of lemon juice, oil and pepper together. Mix in tomatoes and set aside for 5 minutes.

Mix tomato dressing through fennel, then top with tuna and toss well. Garnish with parsley and serve. Serves 6.

# Cauliflower and broccoli salad

 Cauliflower and broccoli are both members of the brassica family of vegetables that aids in detoxification. Serve this salad warm with some grilled fish for a delicious, quick meal.

250g cauliflower, cut into florets
250g broccoli, cut into small florets
1 Lebanese cucumber, diced
2 tablespoons chopped chives
2 tablespoons chopped parsley
1 tablespoon olive oil
1 tablespoon lemon juice
2 teaspoons Dijon-style mustard
½ teaspoon paprika
½ teaspoon pepper

Steam cauliflower for about 6 minutes or until crisp but tender. Steam broccoli for about 5 minutes or until crisp but tender. Cool vegetables to room temperature.

In a large salad bowl, toss cauliflower, broccoli, cucumber, chives and parsley together. In a small screw-top jar, combine oil, lemon juice, mustard, paprika and pepper, and shake until blended.

Mix into salad and toss well. Cover and refrigerate salad for up to 4 hours before serving. Serves 4–6.

# Grilled chicken kebabs

Chicken is used in moderation in the 7 day health and vitality plan as a good source of protein. These kebabs are easy to make, and can be served with the watercress and mushroom salad and boiled rice. They are delicious either hot or at room temperature. Using pine nuts and allspice gives this dish a Moroccan flavour.

500g minced chicken breast
1 clove garlic, crushed
¼ cup pine nuts
1 teaspoon grated lemon rind
3 tablespoons chopped flat-leaf (Italian) parsley
½ teaspoon allspice
½ teaspoon pepper
4 cups warm cooked white rice

Light a charcoal grill or preheat a gas grill. Spray cooking rack with olive oil cooking spray. Soak 8 wooden skewers in water to cover.

In a bowl, mix chicken, garlic, nuts, lemon rind, parsley, allspice and pepper together. Divide into 8 portions and roll each into a sausage shape. Thread onto drained wooden skewers. Spray kebabs with olive oil cooking spray and cook, turning frequently, for about 8–12 minutes or until cooked. Serve immediately on warm cooked rice. Serves 4.

# Spicy baked chicken on saffron rice

Prepare and marinate the chicken during the day so that all the spices penetrate for maximum flavour. Fat-free and skinless chicken is a great source of protein and B vitamins. The dark meat from the chicken contains twice as much iron and zinc as light meat. Buy free-range, organically raised, hormone-free chickens for the best taste and nutrition. They are available from large supermarkets and butchers.

2 teaspoons ground cumin
1 teaspoon turmeric
½ teaspoon chilli powder
1 teaspoon paprika
½ teaspoon cinnamon
3 cloves garlic, crushed
2 tablespoons lemon juice
1 tablespoon olive oil
8 chicken thighs (about 150g each), all skin and fat
    removed

SAFFRON RICE
½ teaspoon powdered saffron or few strands of
    saffron
1 teaspoon olive oil
1 cup long grain rice
2 cups vegetable stock

In a large bowl, combine cumin, turmeric, chilli powder, paprika, cinnamon, garlic, lemon juice and oil. Add chicken pieces, turn well to coat, cover and marinate at room temperature for 45 minutes or up to 4 hours in the refrigerator.

Preheat oven to 200°C. Spray an oven tin with olive oil cooking spray. Spray chicken pieces with olive oil cooking spray and place them in the tin. Bake the chicken for 20 minutes. Turn over chicken pieces and cook for 15–20 minutes or until tender. Meanwhile, make saffron rice. Mix powdered saffron with water or soak saffron strands in water for 10 minutes.

In a medium saucepan, heat oil over medium heat and cook rice for 3 minutes, stirring constantly. Add stock and bring to the boil, stirring occasionally. Reduce heat, cover with a tight-fitting lid and simmer for about 15 minutes until water is absorbed and rice is tender.

Turn off heat, pour saffron mixture over rice and return lid to the saucepan so that the aroma does not escape.

Serve chicken with saffron rice. Serves 4.

# Indian potato and lentil curry

This tasty Indian curry is easy to make and can be served with brown rice for a substantial meal. Ghee or clarified butter is usually used in Indian cuisine but olive oil is used instead in this recipe. Cooked lentils contain iron, potassium, phosphorus and dietary fibre.

2 teaspoons olive oil
1 onion, finely diced
3 cloves garlic, crushed
3 teaspoons fresh grated ginger
1 small red chilli, finely chopped
2 teaspoons curry powder
½ teaspoon cumin seeds
1 cup red lentils (picked over to remove any discoloured ones and rinsed)
2 vine-ripened tomatoes, chopped
2 potatoes, peeled and diced
2½ cups vegetable stock
1 cup frozen peas
2 tablespoons fresh chopped coriander

Over low heat in a large heavy saucepan, heat the oil and sauté the onion for about 10 minutes or until golden brown. Add garlic, ginger and chilli, and sauté on medium heat for 30 seconds. Add the curry powder and cumin seeds, and sauté for 30 seconds. Add the lentils, tomatoes, potatoes and vegetable stock, and bring to the boil, then simmer for about 40–50 minutes or until vegetables and lentils are tender. Stir frequently so that lentils don't stick to the bottom. Stir in peas and cook for 2 minutes. Serve curry garnished with coriander. Serves 4–6.

# Greek chickpea, radish and tomato salad

 Chickpeas are another member of the pulse and lentil family. They are available dried or tinned. To save time you can use the tinned variety, as long as you drain and rinse them thoroughly before using. The tinned variety is used in this recipe. In the 18th century chickpeas were thought to be sexual stimulants. Radishes are another member of the brassica family and in herbal medicine are commonly used for their diuretic effects.

### DRESSING
1 teaspoon Dijon-style mustard
1 tablespoon red-wine vinegar
1 tablespoon olive oil
2 tablespoons lemon juice
½ teaspoon pepper

### SALAD
2 cups cooked chickpeas, well drained
4 radishes, washed and trimmed of roots and
    leaves, and diced
3 vine-ripened tomatoes, chopped
½ red capsicum, seeded, deribbed and diced
½ green capsicum, seeded, deribbed and diced
½ small red (Spanish) onion, peeled and diced
2 tablespoons chopped fresh coriander

In a screw-top jar, combine all dressing ingredients and shake.

In a large bowl, toss together chickpeas, radishes, tomatoes, red capsicum, green capsicum, onion and coriander. Mix dressing into salad and leave to stand for 15 minutes. Serves 2–4.

# Snacks

# Rice cakes with date and fig spread

Rice cakes make a great low-kilojoule snack. They can provide the base for savoury or sweet toppings. Sliced fresh tomato with pepper, or a smear of date and fig spread, makes a delicious tasty treat. Dates and figs are high in dietary fibre, helping to prevent constipation.

1 cup finely chopped dates, pitted
1 cup finely chopped dried figs
¼ cup lemon juice
2 tablespoons fresh orange juice
1 teaspoon grated orange rind
4 rice cakes

In a large bowl, mix dates, figs, lemon juice, orange juice and orange rind together. Cover and leave at room temperature for 2 hours.

Place mixture into the bowl of a food processor fitted with a steel blade or into a blender. Process mixture for about 2 minutes or until it is smooth (if you are using a blender, blend for 1 minute or until mixture is smooth). Store in an airtight container in the refrigerator for up to 2 weeks. Makes 1–1¼ cups.

Spread 2 teaspoons of date and fig spread onto each rice cake. Store remaining spread in the refrigerator.

# Hummus on rice cakes

Hummus is usually made with tahini (a puree of sesame seeds), that is laden with fat. This version is made with yoghurt and makes a delicious savoury snack. Chickpeas are round with a nutty flavour and are used extensively in Middle Eastern cookery. They are a good source of iron, folic acid, vitamin E and dietary fibre.

3 cups tinned chickpeas, plus 1/2 cup from tin liquid
1/4 cup fresh lemon juice
2 cloves garlic, crushed
2 tablespoons natural acidophilus yoghurt
1/4–1/2 teaspoon pepper
1 teaspoon cumin
A few drops of Tabasco
4 rice cakes

In a food processor fitted with the steel blade or in a blender, process chickpeas with 1/2 cup of liquid until smooth, scraping down sides of the bowl. Add lemon juice, garlic, yoghurt, pepper, cumin and Tabasco, and process for 1 minute until the mixture is smooth. Pour mixture into an airtight container and refrigerate until needed. Makes 3 1/4–3 1/2 cups.

Spread 2 teaspoons of hummus onto each rice cake. Store remaining spread in the refrigerator. Serves 2.

# Grilled pineapple with strawberry coulis

Choosing a delicious, juicy pineapple can be a tricky job—look for ones that have a sweet fragrance and ripe appearance. This dish relies on the natural sugars in the pineapple for its sweetness. You can use the indoor griller or the outdoor barbecue to grill the pineapple. Pineapple is a natural appetite suppressant as it contains the enzyme bromelane. Strawberries are a great source of vitamin C and fibre.

1 small ripe pineapple, peeled and cut into 2cm rounds

STRAWBERRY COULIS
10 ripe strawberries, hulled and roughly chopped
1 teaspoon raw honey

Light a charcoal grill or preheat a gas grill. Spray the cooking rack with olive oil spray. Arrange the pineapple on the hot grill and cook for 4–5 minutes on each side. Mash strawberries and pass through a non-reactive sieve (heavy nylon or plastic, not metal). Mix in honey. Serve immediately. Serves 2.

# Warm berries with mango sauce

 In the summertime, berries are at their peak. Blueberries have great antibacterial qualities, and are used to treat diarrhorea and food poisoning, and to help ease stomach upsets. All berries are rich in vitamin C. Raspberry leaf tea also helps with digestive complaints.

½ cup fresh orange juice
1 cup ripe raspberries
1 cup ripe strawberries, hulled and roughly chopped
1 cup ripe blueberries

MANGO SAUCE
1 large ripe mango, peeled, stoned and cubed
2 tablespoons unsweetened pineapple juice or unsweetened orange juice
2 teaspoons fresh lime juice

Heat orange juice in a large non-stick frying pan over low heat. Add raspberries, strawberries and blueberries. Shake pan to turn berries over. Cook for 3 minutes.

Combine mango, pineapple juice and lime juice in a blender or food processor fitted with a steel blade. Blend for about 1 minute or until smooth. Serve immediately with warm berries. Serves 2–3.

# Baked apples with pawpaw sauce

Baked apples taste great, but are often overcooked, making them mushy and fall apart, so be careful with the cooking time. The pawpaw sauce is an excellent sauce of vitamin A and fibre.

4 medium Granny Smith apples, cored to make a
    cavity
4 teaspoons currants
4 teaspoons diced dried apricots
4 teaspoons raw honey
½ teaspoon ground cinnamon
1¼ cups unsweetened apple juice

PAWPAW SAUCE
350g ripe pawpaw, pitted and cubed
2 teaspoons fresh lime juice
4 sprigs fresh mint

Preheat oven to 180°C.

Place apples in an ovenproof dish. Put 1 teaspoon of currants and 1 teaspoon of apricots into each cavity, and drizzle each one with 1 teaspoon of honey. Sprinkle each apple with cinnamon. Pour the apple juice around the apples. Cover dish loosely with aluminium foil and bake for 50–60 minutes or until the apples are tender when pierced with a fork. Remove dish from the oven and set aside for 5 minutes.

Remove the juice from the pan and place into a blender or food processor fitted with a steel blade. Add the pawpaw and lime juice, and blend for 1 minute or until the mixture is smooth.

Serve baked apples with pawpaw sauce and garnish with fresh sprigs of mint. Serves 4.

# Raspberry flummery in almond and date crust

 This rich, sweet snack can be served any time of the day. Raspberry flummery gives a luscious sweetness and provides good sources of vitamins, minerals and fibre. Making the crust mixture can be a time consuming job but it is well worth the effort.

1½ cups chopped raw almonds
2 cups chopped pitted dates

FILLING
1 sachet (4½g) low kilojoule raspberry flavoured
    jelly crystals
1 cup boiling water
½ cup cold water
1 cup ripe raspberries plus 8 raspberries for
    decoration
2 tablespoons natural acidophilus yoghurt

On a cutting board, chop the almonds and dates together for about 5 minutes or until they are well combined. Knead the mixture together. Press mixture into the bottom and sides of a 21cm pie dish. Refrigerate crust for 30 minutes.

Meanwhile, prepare the filling. In a large bowl, mix

jelly crystals with boiling water until crystals dissolve. Add cold water and cool jelly to room temperature.

Mash raspberries and pass through a non-reactive sieve (heavy nylon or plastic, not metal). Mix raspberry puree and yogurt into jelly. Refrigerate the filling until it is nearly set, about 45 minutes to 1 hour.

Transfer the filling into a mixing bowl and beat in an electric mixer for about 10 minutes, or until the mixture is light and fluffy. Pour mixture into the pie crust and refrigerate for about 2 hours or until filling is set. Decorate with raspberries and serve. Makes 8 slices.

# Banana cream pie

You will see how easy it is to make the almond and date crust for this banana cream pie, and to make creative fillings. The almond and date mixture can be rolled into walnut-size pieces, and refrigerated and used as an energy booster. Silken tofu is available at supermarkets and in Asian stores. Raw honey is available from health-food shops.

ALMOND AND DATE CRUST
1½ cups chopped raw almonds
2 cups chopped pitted dates

FILLING
300g silken tofu
1 tablespoon raw honey
2 ripe bananas, peeled
½ ripe mango, peeled and chopped
2 teaspoons lemon juice
2 teaspoons grated lemon rind
1 teaspoon grated orange rind

On a cutting board, chop the almonds and dates together for about 5 minutes or until they are well combined. Knead the mixture together. Press mixture into the bottom and sides of a 21cm pie dish.

Refrigerate crust for 30 minutes.

Meanwhile, in the bowl of a food processor fitted with a steel blade or in a blender, process tofu, honey, bananas, mango, lemon juice, lemon rind and orange rind until the mixture is smooth.

Pour mixture into prepared crust and refrigerate for 4 hours or until it is set. Makes 8 slices.

# Spicy popcorn snack

Popcorn is a great source of fibre and potassium, and it is gluten-free. It is a filling snack, and can be eaten instead of fat-filled potato chips, corn chips or roasted, salted nuts. This snack can only be made in an air popcorn maker and is best eaten immediately after you make it.

¼ cup raw popping corn
1 teaspoon olive oil
½ teaspoon curry powder
⅛ teaspoon cayenne pepper
½ teaspoon paprika

Make popcorn in an air popcorn maker.

In a large bowl, mix together olive oil, curry powder, cayenne pepper and paprika. Add popcorn and mix well. Serve immediately. Serves 2.

# Hiking mix

This nutritious snack can be prepared and portioned into 7 small bags for the week. Do not eat more than 1 portion a day, as the nuts provide too many kilojoules if too much is eaten. Hiking mix is an excellent supply of vitamin E, potassium, magnesium and fibre, which helps in the 7 day health and vitality plan.

1 cup raw walnuts, roughly chopped
½ cup raw almonds
½ cup raw cashew nuts
¼ cup sunflower seeds
½ cup sultanas
½ cup dried apricots, cut in half
½ cup dried dates, pitted and cut in half

In a large bowl, mix nuts, seeds and fruit together. Portion mixture into 7 plastic bags. Store in an airtight container.

# Orange mango jelly cups

Here is an old-time favourite, usually served at children's birthday parties. These snacks are perfect for any time of the day when you need a sweet pick-me-up. As they are made with low kilojoule jelly crystals, they are also guilt-free if you eat one too many.

> 3 large thick-skinned oranges, cut in half horizontally
> 1 sachet (4½g) orange mango flavour low kilojoule jelly crystals
> 1 cup boiling water
> ½ cup cold water
> 1 large ripe mango (about 500g), peeled, stoned and cubed

Carefully remove all the flesh from the orange halves, leaving the white pulp intact.

In a large bowl, mix jelly crystals with boiling water and stir to dissolve crystals. Add cold water and refrigerate for 30 minutes. Stir in mango cubes and refrigerate for 15 minutes.

Carefully fill orange cups with jelly mixture and refrigerate for about 2 hours or until jelly is firm. Serves 6.

# Ginger apple fizz

 This sparkling drink is refreshing and delicious. Ginger aids digestion and is a great remedy for nausea, including travel sickness.

1x4cm piece fresh ginger, peeled and quartered
1 golden delicious apple, washed, cored and
    quartered
1 red delicious apple, washed, cored and
    quartered
1 cup mineral water
Ice cubes

In a juice extractor, first process the ginger, then the apples. Mix in mineral water and serve in chilled glasses over ice. Serves 2.

# Watermelon surprise

Watermelon is a great fruit—its high water content stimulates the kidneys to work more efficiently, and so it is a natural diuretic. In the summertime, watermelon is at its peak, and is cheap and plentiful. Its seeds are believed to have a high concentration of diuretic properties and the rind contains chlorophyll, a blood purifier.

   500g watermelon, rind scrubbed clean
   1 tablespoon fresh lime juice

Cut the watermelon into pieces that will fit through the juice extractor's feed tube. Process the watermelon. Mix in lime juice and serve immediately. Serves 2.

# Cherry cooler

For a 'spring cleaning' any time of the year, drink this tasty cherry cooler to flush the kidneys of built-up toxins. This juice can be quite beneficial for people who suffer from skin problems due to the accumulation of waste matter in their digestive system.

1 red apple, washed, cored and quartered
1 cup pitted cherries
¼ small ripe pineapple, peeled, cored and
    chopped
4 ice cubes, crushed

In a juice extractor, process first the apple, then the cherries and pineapple.

Pour the cherry cooler into chilled glasses over crushed ice. Serves 2.

# Frozen cherry and yoghurt delights

This snack is very easy to make and delicious to eat. If the taste is too sour for you, add a little more honey to the mixture to sweeten it. You can also use fresh pureed mangoes, apricots, raspberries, strawberries or blueberries. Cherries have a diuretic effect and help to cleanse the kidneys of toxins.

> ½ cup water
> 3 strips orange rind
> 1 stick cinnamon
> 1 cup cherries, pitted
> ½ cup natural acidophilus yoghurt
> 1 teaspoon honey

In a saucepan, heat water, orange rind and cinnamon stick over medium heat for 1 minute. Add cherries, cover saucepan with a tight-fitting lid and bring to the boil. Lower heat to a simmer and cook for about 5–8minutes or until fruit is just cooked. Remove from heat and cool to room temperature. Drain cherries in a colander.

Puree cherries in a blender until they are smooth. Mix in yoghurt and honey. Fill an ice block maker—ice block makers are usually plastic with 4 compartments to pour the liquid into. Fill to 1cm below the rim, and insert 4 sticks after filling. Freeze for about 4 hours or until frozen.

# Recipe index